THE RAF AT 100

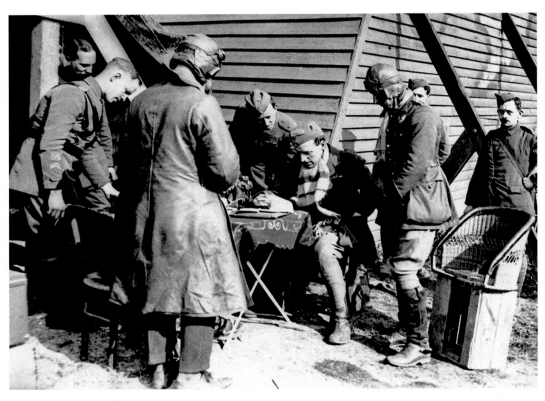

RAF pilots report the
position of enemy troops
on the Western Front,
April 1918.

THE RAF AT 100

A CENTURY IN PHOTOGRAPHS

mirrorpix

The
History
Press

All images are available to purchase from
www.vintagephotosonline.co.uk

Cover illustrations. Front: Spitfire F Mk XIIs of No. 41
Squadron based at RAF Friston, Sussex. Back: Daily Herald
photographer in the cockpit of a Folland Gnat aircraft of
the Red Arrows.

First published 2017
This edition published 2021

The History Press
The Mill, Brimscombe Port
Stroud, Gloucestershire, GL5 2QG
www.thehistorypress.co.uk

British Library Cataloguing in Publication Data.
A catalogue record for this book is available from the British
Library.

ISBN 978 0 7509 9477 4

Typesetting and origination by The History Press
Printed and bound in Europe by Imak.

FOREWORD

On 1 April 1918, the Royal Flying Corps and the Royal Naval Air Service were amalgamated to form the Royal Air Force. This newly merged organisation, combining the might of the Royal Navy with the military, was created to monitor the skies of the British Empire and planned to fall under the command of the British Government Air Ministry. It seemed a sensible response to the horrors of the First World War, but for all its power the nascent RAF had a rocky start, suffering defence cuts and intense scrutiny from some quarters as to whether it was needed at all.

The Second World War changed the picture considerably and the RAF rapidly came to be regarded as vital an organisation to the survival of the British nation as the Royal Navy was on the seas, its worth surely proven beyond all doubt by the Battle of Britain that raged across the summer of 1940. Throughout subsequent conflicts the RAF has continually evolved to meet the needs of the age at hand, whether through the nuclear threat of the Cold War to the modern-day struggles fighting insurgents in the harsh terrain of deserts and mountains.

This impressive collection of photographs presents the varied history of the RAF across 100 years. Collated from the incredible Mirrorpix photographic archive, home to one of the world's largest photographic libraries with over 100 million images and more than a century of news coverage, the photographs in this book chart the changes in mood and role, aircraft and personnel across a century of war and peace. From early biplanes through to the pioneering era of the 1920s and '30s, from the jet age and the Cold War to Iraq and Afghanistan, these beautiful photographs showcase the remarkable history of the RAF during its lifetime.

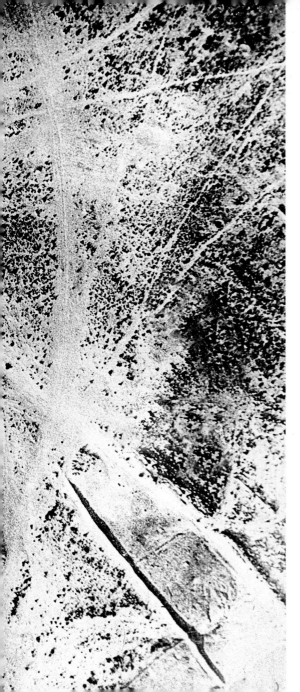

RAF aerial photograph of a bomb bursting close to a fort on the Palestine Front, *c.* June 1918.

An RAF Handley Page H.P.
O/400 bomber with its
wings folded back is pulled
across a French aerodrome,
September 1918.

A Sopwith Camel of
the RAF credited with
shooting down over 1,200
enemy aircraft during
the war. It also served as
a ground-attack aircraft,
especially towards the end
of the conflict, c. 1918.

Mr Aviation himself, Thomas Sopwith in October 1921. His aircraft had a massive influence on the outcome of both world wars, not to mention several lesser conflicts. From the Sopwith Camel to the Hawker Hurricane, he dominated the skies across the globe.

De Havilland DH4 aircraft
at the Hendon air display,
27 June 1925.

The RAF delivering mail during the May 1926 general strike. With large numbers of workers on strike, the government enlisted the help of the armed services and volunteers to maintain essential services.

Prince George gets out of the cockpit of an RAF plane after flying to Hull, East Yorkshire, October 1929.

A Supermarine S.6A, one of the aircraft taking part in the Isle of Man Schneider Trophy Race, seen here in operation by the RAF in the Solent.

On 5 October 1930, the R101 (the largest airship in the world at that time) crashed in France during its maiden overseas voyage; only seven of the fifty-four people on board survived. Standing by the wreck of the R101, rescue workers hold the tattered remains of an RAF flag.

Prime Minister Ramsay
MacDonald climbing aboard
a Fairey 3F aircraft of number
24 Squadron on 25 October
1930. MacDonald had been
attending the Imperial Air
Conference at Croydon before
boarding his flight to RAF
Halton, where he travelled on
by car to Chequers.

Lord Trenchard (right) with
Sir S. Hoare (centre) and Air
Vice Marshal Halahan after
the foundation stone of a
new RAF college was laid
at Cranwell, Lincolnshire,
July 1935.

Hawker Fury IIs of
25 Squadron, 1937.

An RAF Gloster Gauntlet II crashes into the back garden of a house in Edmonton, London, December 1937. The pilot, who was flying from Kenley to Digby in Lincolnshire, escaped uninjured.

Part of the nation's effort for 'preparedness' was the huge bombing instruction station at Acklington, Northumberland, which, having been closed since 1920, reopened in 1938. This photograph, taken on 13 April 1938, gives you an impression of the size of this important RAF centre.

➤ A Fairey Swordfish of the Fleet Air Arm comes into land on the flight deck of HMS *Ark Royal*, c. 1938.

Mk 1 Supermarine Spitfires
flying in traditional Vic
formation on 5 May 1939,
just before the outbreak of
the Second World War.

RAF pilots and crew make their way to their Avro Anson planes, September 1939.

A squadron of RAF Vickers
Wellington Mk I bombers,
c. 1939.

RAF pilots scramble during
the Battle of Britain conflict.

◄ An RAF spitfire pilot of 603 Squadron inspects the identity crest and nickname 'Scottie' on the side of his plane, 1941.

➤ Supermarine Spitfire Mk Vb of No. 92 Squadron, the East India Squadron, pictured in flight on 19 May 1941.

◄ Two members of the Women's Auxiliary Air Force (WAAF) had a fight on their hands with an errant barrage balloon, c. May 1941. Women were drafted into the WAAF as a means of freeing up men to fight for the RAF. They were mainly employed to help maintain Britain's air defences.

▲ A scene in the RAF Operations Room at Headquarters Fighter Command, Bentley Priory, Middlesex, June 1941. Radiolocation was used during the Second World War to locate enemy aircraft. The radiolocator's messages, and those of the Royal Observer Corps, were communicated instantly to RAF Operations Rooms, where they were plotted on large table maps. The radiolocators were maintained by highly skilled radio mechanics and manned by RAF and Women's Auxiliary Air Force radio operators.

A Lancaster bomber
crewman screws a nose-art
painting of Zola on to the
side of his aircraft for good
luck, 1942.

A member of the Women's
Auxiliary Air Force tows
an RAF Hudson bomber
and its crew back to their
dispersal following a mission
over Germany, c. 1942.

Women's Auxiliary Air Force and RAF ground crew roller skating at their station, June 1942. A Westland Lysander communication aircraft can be seen in the background.

◄ A Women's Auxiliary Air Force officer packing a parachute for RAF pilots to use during one of the bombing raids in June 1942.

➤ RAF crews arrive at their dispersal point, driven by a Women's Auxiliary Air Force officer who lends a hand with their tuck boxes, June 1942.

Women's Auxiliary Air Force cooks are busy filling up vacuum flasks with coffee, tea and Bovril for the RAF pilots and crew to take on their bombing raids, June 1942.

A member of the Women's Auxiliary Air Force on a tractor pulling a load of 1,000lb bombs at an RAF base, 1942.

◄ Wrens (members of
the Women's Royal Naval
Service) placing a wireless
in a Westland Lysander at
a Royal Navy Air Station in
England, September 1942.

▲ RAF Lancaster bomber
on display in Trafalgar
Square, London, for Wings
for Victory week, March
1943.

RAF Lancaster bomber
being assembled by RAF
and Women's Auxiliary Air
Force officers for display in
Trafalgar Square, London,
for Wings for Victory week,
March 1943.

Flight Sergeant Wimpy
was the Welsh Collie
mascot of the Women's
Auxiliary Air Force band
at an RAF station in the
west of England. He had
just been enrolled in the
newly formed allied forces
Mascot Club of the People's
Dispensary for Sick Animals,
September 1943.

Aerial view of the devastation caused following the attack by 617 Squadron, the Dambusters, on the night of 16–17 May 1943 on the Möhne and Eder dams in the Ruhr Valley, Germany. The raids caused catastrophic flooding.

Seven Spitfire F Mk XIIs, fitted with Rolls-Royce Griffon engines, of No. 41 Squadron based at RAF Friston, Sussex, pictured in formation over the South Downs on 12 April 1944.

The latest Avro Lancaster III bomber plane, fitted with Merlin 28 engines, pictured in April 1944.

Pilots of No. 132 Squadron next to Spitfire LF Mk IX at RAF Ford. The pilots had just flown the first Spitfire offensive sortie over Germany between Aachen and Cologne, firing on Nazi fighters and gliders, railway wagons and locomotives before returning to base without loss on 25 April 1944.

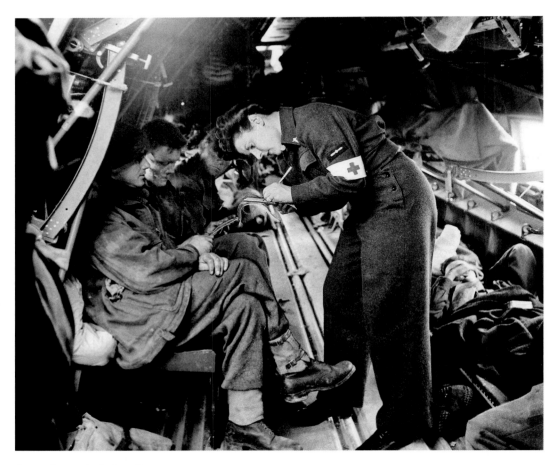

A nursing orderly, Leading
Aircraftwoman P. Bradburn,
attending to wounded
soldiers on their return
from Normandy, France,
July 1944.

Spitfire PR Mk XI being
flown by Jeffrey Quill,
Vickers-Supermarine's chief
test pilot, on a test flight on
13 July 1944. The PR Mk XIs
were photoreconnaissance
aircraft designed to operate
at high altitudes (over
30,000ft), as well as at high
speeds (over 400mph).

A Handley Page Halifax
No. 6 Group of RAF
Bomber Command flying
over the target during a
daylight raid on the oil
refinery at Wanne-Eickel
in the Ruhr, Germany,
12 October 1944.

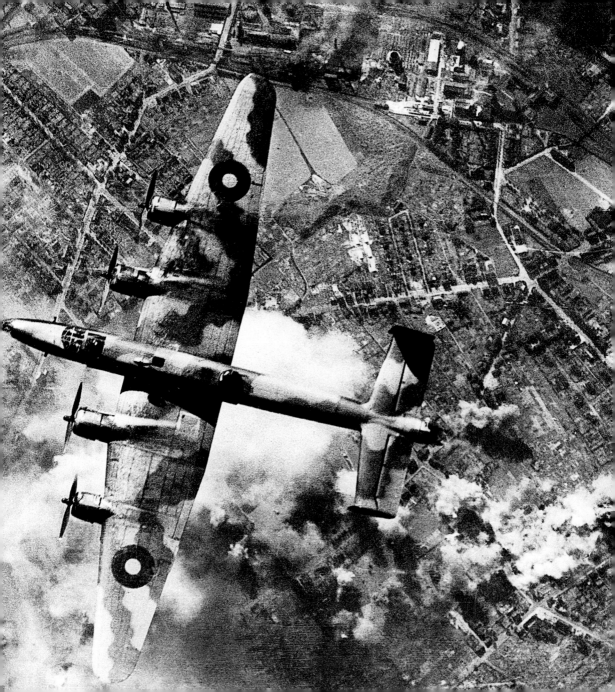

Bomber Command load one of
the new 12,000lb 'earthquake'
bombs onto a Lancaster II
bomber on 14 October 1944.
They were the same bombs
that sunk the 45,000-ton
German battleship *Tirpitz*
in Norway.

An RAF Lancaster bomber, its outline blurred through the haze of fires, is seen taking off between two bands of flame as the fog is dispersed, May 1945. This is one of the first official photographs to be released of Fog Investigation and Dispersal Operation (FIDO) in action. FIDO was used during the Second World War for dispersing fog from an airfield.

RAF Fighter Pilot Douglas Bader attending a party, 29 May 1945. Bader was one of Britain's great heroes of the Second World War; from June 1940 to August 1941, the flying ace downed twenty-two German planes. As a Spitfire squadron commander, Bader rewrote aerial combat, introducing the tactic of flying at very high altitude and then thundering down on the Luftwaffe planes, guns blazing, as well as proving that larger squadrons of Spitfires would be more effective.

Manchester folk, proud of
the city's wonder-bomber,
flocked to Piccadilly in
their thousands to see a
Lancaster bomber on a War
Savings campaign in August
1945.

Thanksgiving flight over London: 'Tin-Legs' Group Captain Douglas Bader – the immortal leader in many a battle – climbs into the cockpit and prepares to lead the flypast, 15 September 1945.

Group Captain H.J. Wilson walks away from a Gloster Meteor, in which he hopes to break the air-speed record, October 1945. The Gloster Meteor was the first jet aircraft to enter service with the RAF.

An Avro York aircraft of RAF Transport Command seen here unloading on the apron of Berlin's Gatow airfield, c. 1948. In the foreground food supplies, which had been flown in earlier in the day to break the Soviet blockade, await distribution.

Goods loaded onto a British aircraft for the Berlin Air Lift during the Russian blockade of the city, November 1948.

Supermarine Spitfire F22s,
of RAF Ouston, in flight
rehearsing for the 10th
anniversary 'Battle of Britain'
display, 27 August 1950.

Pilots scramble to their
Meteor jet aircraft at
Church Fenton RAF Station,
North Yorkshire, at the
opening of Exercise Pinnacle,
a period of armament
training, October 1951.

A Vampire jet being brought out of the hangar in readiness for flight, April 1951. No. 613 Squadron (City of Manchester) of the Royal Auxiliary Air Force was the first to go into action under the government's new scheme for fitting auxiliary squadrons into the defence programme.

The first British-produced jet bomber, the English Electric Canberra B2, makes its first test flight at Farnborough Airshow, September 1952.

The advanced jet trainer, the Folland Gnat, being introduced to the press at RAF Valley, Anglesey, 1953.

The Queen and Prince
Philip enjoy the flypast,
pointing out the RAF
Canberras to Prince
Charles and Princess Anne,
at the Trooping the Colour
ceremony on 11 June 1953.

Queen Elizabeth II
inspecting the RAF Guard
of Honour at Runnymede
Memorial, Surrey,
17 October 1953.

Air Officer Commanding
visit to RAF Sutton on Hull,
East Yorkshire, where they
are observing auxiliary
personnel at work, 1 January
1955.

Royal Auxiliary Air Force
Flying Officer Eric Lloyd
of Eccleston and Leading
Aircraftwoman Peggy Hughes
of Tottington keep track of an
invader on a radar screen at
3613 Fighter Control Unit at
Bowlee, 11 February 1955.

Five RAF Javelins on the tarmac with their jet engines being fired up at RAF Odiham, Hampshire, 2 July 1956. The Gloster Javelin, an all-weather interceptor, was the first ever delta-wing aircraft to enter service with any air force in the world.

A nose view of the RAF's all-weather fighter, the Gloster Javelin, showing the two huge jet intakes and the unusually wide undercarriage, Farnborough Airshow, 3 September 1956.

Fairey Delta 2 jet fighter
at Farnborough Airshow,
3 September 1956, which
broke the world speed
record in March of the
same year.

An RAF Avro Vulcan
bomber takes off at
the 'Flying Display
and Exhibition' of
the Society of British
Aircraft Constructors at
Farnborough Airshow on
3 September 1956.

Paratroopers of the
3rd Battalion prepare
to embark on an RAF
Shackleton Aircraft at
Blackbushe Airfield, bound
for Cyprus, 1956.

RAF ground crew loading
bombs onto Canberras on
an airfield in Cyprus, 1956.

▲ Emergency in Malaya, 29 October 1959. Speed of movement was essential in combating the communist insurgents in the Malayan jungle and helicopters played a vital part.

➤ Children at play on Bridlington Sands are thrilled at the sight of an RAF helicopter swooping over the beach and a man being swiftly lowered to the beach – all part of a practice rescue operation in July 1960. This is a rare sight, for rescue helicopters would not normally land survivors on the beach, except in emergency.

RAF ground crew fuelling the missile with hydrogen peroxide and kerosene at RAF Scampton on the missile's debut to the press, 14 February 1963. The Avro Blue Steel – a British air-launched, rocket-propelled nuclear stand-off missile, built to arm the V-bomber force – was the primary British nuclear deterrent weapon of the 1960s.

Fylingdales Royal Air Force
Station on Snod Hill in the
North York Moors. A radar
base and part of the United
States-controlled Ballistic
Missile Early Warning
System, 1963.

Five Hawker Hunter fighters take off at RAF Wittering, Peterborough, 16 July 1963.

Handley Page Victor
bomber with Blue Steel
atomic missile at RAF
Wittering, Peterborough,
February 1964.

A Blue Steel bomb being
loaded into the bomb bay
of a Handley Page Victor,
February 1964.

Vulcan bomber, 1964.

An English Electric Lightning
T5 of RAF 111 Squadron,
April 1964, taking off with
Chief Marshall Sir Wallace
Kyle on board on the day
that Bomber Command and
Fighter Command merged
to form Strike Command.

A bird's-eye view of the Farnborough Airshow in September 1964 – the first show for two years – taken from a Westland Widgeon helicopter. The camouflaged aircraft in the foreground are a Victor (left) and a Vulcan (right).

A Blue Steel missile about
to be loaded into the
bombing bay of a Victor
bomber, RAF Wittering,
1964.

Hawker Siddeley Kestrel vertical take-off and landing jet trials, 1965. The Kestrel was the forerunner of the Harrier jump jet.

2nd Battalion, Parachute Regiment, being briefed in January 1965 before leaving RAF Lyneham, Wiltshire, to support Malaysia in a border struggle with Indonesia.

The view from the cockpit
of a Red Arrow as they fly
over RAF Little Rissington,
Gloucestershire, home of
the Central Flying School,
in formation on 4 August
1965.

Daily Herald photographer Ron Burton in the cockpit of a Folland Gnat aircraft of the RAF Aerobatics Team, the Red Arrows, as he joins the team on a training flight over the Central Flying School at RAF Little Rissington, Gloucestershire, 4 August 1965.

An RAF Lockheed C-130
Hercules Mk 1 aircraft
from 36 Squadron at
RAF Lyneham, Wiltshire,
26 September 1967. The
aircraft had just entered
service with the RAF.

The Hawker Siddeley Harrier, the
world's first operational vertical
take-off close-support fighter,
pictured at Dunsfold Airfield, Surrey,
for a demonstration on 4 January
1968. The plane is now in quantity
production and is among the first of
sixty Harriers for the RAF.

◄ Prince Charles sitting
at the controls of an
aircraft at RAF Oakington,
Cambridgeshire, on his 21st
birthday, November 1969.

▲ Queen Elizabeth II, the
Queen Mother and Prince
Charles visit the Central
Flying School at RAF Little
Rissington, Gloucestershire,
1969.

Prince Charles and his
father Prince Philip
wearing RAF uniform at
the passing out parade at
RAF Cranwell, Lincolnshire,
September 1971.

Two RAF Westland
Whirlwind helicopters
at RAF Boulmer,
Northumberland,
24 October 1974. The
aircraft in the foreground is a
search and rescue helicopter.

A British RAF Harrier jet is camouflaged and ready for action, near Belize City, Belize. The British Armed Forces are in Belize in the run up to independence, should the Guatemalans invade, March 1978.

The last serving RAF
Lancaster bomber making
its first flight on 7 May
1979 at Staverton Airshow
after having been grounded
nearly two years previously
for a major overhaul.

The RAF's Red Arrows team at RAF Bitteswell, Leicestershire, on 15 November 1979 alongside the new BAE Systems Hawk aircraft, which were to be used for the first time for the 1980 season. The Hawk was to replace the Folland Gnat, which had been with the Red Arrows since its formation in 1964.

The Welsh Guards of RAF
Brize Norton, Oxfordshire,
are welcomed home from
the Falklands in July 1982.
Prince Charles was there to
meet them.

The first group of women
from the Women's Royal
Army Corps to join
servicemen and army
nurses in the Falkland
Islands leaves from RAF
Brize Norton, Oxfordshire,
July 1983.

The Spitfire at the
entrance gates
to RAF Brawdy,
Pembrokeshire,
being taken away
for reconstruction,
5 November 1984.

A reunion in July 1986
for Spitfire workers who
assembled the wings of the
iconic British fighter planes
at a factory in Newhall
Street, central Birmingham,
during 1941 and 1942.
The women at the factory
worked seven days a week
for £4, including bonuses.

An RAF Lockheed C-130
Hercules transport plane
seen taxiing on the tarmac
in the Middle East during
the Gulf War, 23 January
1991.

◄ A machine gunner
on board an RAF Puma
helicopter from Ali Al Salem
Air Base, Kuwait, on patrol
near the Iraqi border during
the Iraq War, March 2003.

▲ British marines from
40 Commando enter Basra,
Iraq, by RAF helicopters
during the Iraq War, April
2003.

Prince William is taken for a ride in a Hawk aircraft while on work experience at RAF Valley, Anglesey, December 2005.

▲ Navigator Jim Roughton of 617 Squadron, the Dambusters, pictured leaving his GR4 Tornado at Kandahar Airfield, Afghanistan, December 2013.

➤ Actor Kenneth More and actress Susannah York sitting on a Spitfire at RAF Duxford, Cambridgeshire, with technical advisers during a break in the filming of the *Battle of Britain*, 1 June 1968.

A Spitfire on a flypast over
the ruins of Coventry
Cathedral to commemorate
the bombing of the city
during the Second World
War, 13 September 1990.

A Spitfire swoops over
Coopers Field for Cardiff
Armed Forces Day, 27 June
2009.

◄ A Lancaster bomber flies over Derwent Reservoir in Derbyshire on the seventieth anniversary of the Dambuster's raid, May 2013.

▲ Bomber Command veteran John Hall, aged 94, served as a flight lieutenant during the Second World War. He flew sixty missions as a tail gunner in a Lancaster bomber across two tours of duty from 1940 to 1944 – a remarkable feat, considering the average survival rate for tail gunners was around four missions.

⋏ RAF Aerobatic Team,
the Red Arrows, in their
HS Gnat trainer aircraft,
August 1967.

➤ The Red Arrows, June
2004.

The Red Arrows open
Farnborough Airshow,
14 June 2014.

The Red Arrows perform
at Eastbourne Airbourne
Airshow in East Sussex,
August 2014.

◄ The Red Arrows in perfect symmetry at Eastbourne Airbourne Airshow in East Sussex, August 2014.

➤ The Red Arrows perform at Sunderland International Airshow, held at Seaburn beachfront, 25 July 2015.

The Red Arrows fly over the *Queen Mary 2* as part of Cunard's 175th anniversary celebrations in Liverpool, 4 July 2015.

◄ Prince William and Prince Harry at their helicopter training base, RAF Shawbury, Shropshire, 2009.

➤ Crowds gather on The Mall, London, as the RAF perform a flypast of Buckingham Palace after the wedding of Prince William and Catherine Middleton, 29 April 2011.

RAF Tornado pilots relax at their base in Kuwait after their bombing missions over Iraq are cancelled, 20 December 1998. Operation Desert Fox was a major four-day bombing campaign on Iraqi targets from 16–19 December 1998 by the US and UK.

An RAF Tornado jet being prepared for battle in the hangar at Ali Al Salem Air Base in Kuwait during the joint UK and US bombing campaign of Iraqi targets, code-named Operation Desert Fox, December 1998. These strikes were officially undertaken in response to Iraq's failure to comply with United Nations Security Council resolutions as well as their interference with United Nations Special Commission inspectors.

Sergeant Anna Irwin, a loadmaster and rear gunner on Boeing Chinooks, pictured in Kandahar, Afghanistan, on 1 December 2007.

RAF Chinook crew members at Camp Bastion, Helmand Province, Afghanistan, on 1 December 2007. Left to right: Sergeant Anna Irwin, Sergeant Liz Mcconagh, Squadron Leader Paul Curnow, Flight Lieutenant Mike Killick and Flight Sergeant Sam Norris.

RAF Typhoon Eurofighters landing after a sortie over Libya at Gioia del Colle Air Base, Southern Italy, 2010.

A tornado jet from 617
Squadron, famously
known as the Dambusters,
before being deployed to
Afghanistan.

Flight Lieutenant Robbie Low (right) and Flight Lieutenant Jon Nixon (left) of 12 Squadron at RAF Lossiemouth, Scotland, board a G4 Tornado for an operation in Kandahar, Afghanistan, August 2009.

The first all-woman
RAF Merlin combat
crew, RAF Benson,
Oxfordshire, 2009.